Great Smoky Mountains National Park

THE RANGE OF LIFE

by

Rose Houk

GREAT SMOKY MOUNTAINS ASSOCIATION

©2000, ©2002, ©2003 Great Smoky Mountains Association
Edited by Kent Cave and Steve Kemp
Designed by Christina Watkins
Typography and Production by Triad Associates
Printed in Hong Kong

8 9 10 11 12 13 14 15

ISBN 0-937207-29-2

Great Smoky Mountains Association is a private, nonprofit organization
which supports the educational, scientific, and historical programs of Great
Smoky Mountains National Park. Our publications are an educational
service intended to enhance the public's understanding and enjoyment of
the national park. If you would like to know more about our publications,
memberships, guided hikes and other projects, please contact: Great Smoky
Mountains Association, 115 Park Headquarters Road, Gatlinburg, TN
37738 (865) 436-7318
www.SmokiesInformation.org

ACKNOWLEDGMENTS
The author extends deep gratitude to the Great Smoky Mountains
Association for the opportunity to do this book, especially Steve Kemp for
his unwavering good humor and keen publishing acumen. The artistry of
Christina Watkins graces every page, along with the vision of the many talented photographers who captured the lush beauty and life of these grand
old mountains. Bill Stiver and Rebecca Vial loaned valuable time and assis-
tance, as did those who had the patience to review the manuscript: Janet
Rock, Kim Delozier, Kent Cave, and Art Schultz. Working in the Smoky
Mountains is always a pleasure because of the open arms of friends
Annette and John Hartigan. Unending thanks to the unknown camper
who directed my attention to the river otters in Abrams Creek. And finally, to the memory of my father, Robert Houk, whose lifelong encourage-
ment and support kept me on the path.

PHOTOGRAPHY CREDITS
Willard Clay: 9 top, 30 (showy orchis), 31 (violets), 43; Michael Collier:
cover (logs), 6 (headstone), 16 (snail), 27 (partridge berry, lichen), 30
(bloodroot), 45 top; Bill Duyck: 18 (hummingbird, hooded warbler), 19
(black-chinned red salamander), 21, 25 (mouse), 27 (bird), 31 (sunflower);
George H.H. Huey: 15 top; George Humphries: 5, 6 (mountains), 7, 8, 23,
24 (inset), 25 (redbud, mushrooms, beech, maples), 26 (forest), 28, 30
(asters. squirrel corn), 31 (farm, coneflower), 32, 35, 36 (bridge, bottom),
38, 39 (Mouse Creek, Rainbow and Grotto Falls), 41; Adam Jones: cover
(Smokies), 6 (bottom), 11 (sumac), 15 (cub), 16 (cardinal, snake, spider),
18 (Nashville Warbler, bluebird, bobwhite, Screech Owl, waxwing), 19
(red-cheeked salamander), 20 (foxes), 22 (top, dogwood), 26 (hawk), 29
(bird, orchid), 30 (columbine, fire pink), 31 (lily), 33 (rhododendron), 34
(frog, dragonfly), 36 (top), 37, 39 (bird), 40 (top, stream, spider), 42
(church), 45 (barn, cabin), 46 (farm), 48, inside back cover, back cover
(Smokies); Mary Ann Kressig: 9 (snow), 12 (bear carving), 14 (bear with
cub), 24 (forest), 30 (girls), 39 (girls), 42 top, 45 (spring house), 46
(church); Bill Lea: 6 (top), 10, 11 (berries, acorns, bear, squawroot), 12
(track), 14 (hornet nest, digging bear, three bears, bottom), 16 (raccoon),
17, 19 (newt), 20 (bobcat), 22 (woodpecker), 29 (Jack-in-the-pulpit,
hiker), 34 (trillium), 36 (moss), 40 (fisherman); National Park Service: all
historic photographs; Pat O'Hara: inside front cover, page 1, 2, 9 (lichen,
flower, Charlies Bunion), 27 (road, mushrooms), 29 (top, path), 30
(Solomon's seal, foamflower, spiderwort, phacelia), 31 (both lady's slippers,
iris, violet), 33 (inset, azaleas); J. Heidecker/Vireo: 40 (kingfisher); Ken
Wilson: 20 (elk).

ILLUSTRATION CREDITS
John Dawson: page 11, 22.

Contents

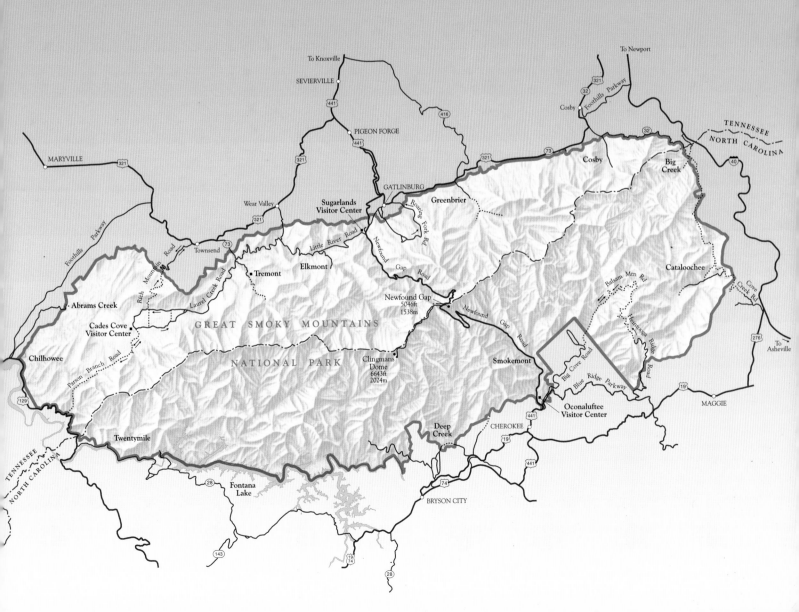

Spurs, Knobs, and Leads

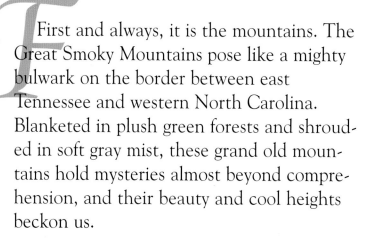

For early residents, mountain geology presented both obstacles and opportunities. TOP: *traveling Newfound Gap Road.* RIGHT: *a grave marker carved from native stone.*

A good view of the Great Smoky Mountains is always inspirational. ABOVE: *view from the Foothills Parkway.* RIGHT: *walkway to the observation tower atop Clingmans Dome.*

First and always, it is the mountains. The Great Smoky Mountains pose like a mighty bulwark on the border between east Tennessee and western North Carolina. Blanketed in plush green forests and shrouded in soft gray mist, these grand old mountains hold mysteries almost beyond comprehension, and their beauty and cool heights beckon us.

Drive up toward Clingmans Dome, the highest peak in the Smokies. That part's easy. Then park the family carriage and get out and walk the last steep half-mile on the paved trail, up the spiral ramp to the top of the lookout tower. If the clouds have lifted, from this supreme summit 6,643 feet above sea level, you'll be treated to a bird's-eye view in all directions. Stand and study the scene for a while and nothing will make sense.

The lay of the land in these mountains is a convoluted puzzle. The terrain seems not to obey any discernible, orderly pattern. These mountains are a chaos of geography and geology. And they appear impenetrable.

A mainline ridge marks the boundary of the park's two shared states. From this central spine a welter of lesser pinnacles, spurs, and knobs sprawls out in every direction like unruly vertebrae. Their steep flanks are

separated by drainages — called branches, prongs, and hollows in these parts — that tumble to the river valleys.

A geographer will say this about the Smokies: They are part of the Appalachian Highlands, a long belt of elevated country that stretches from Virginia to Georgia. On the Tennessee side, the range "projects in ramparts and massive bastions above much lower foothills." On the North Carolina side "the mountain front is poorly defined, and the innumerable sharp-crested spurs branch out from the main divide."

The streams sometimes misbehave. Many start in western North Carolina and "flow in a curious fashion westward through the mountain barrier to join the Tennessee River."

A geologist will say this: These mountains are old. The rock that forms their foundation is about a billion years old, give or take. It's hard rock — gneisses, schists, and granites — with gorgeous crystalline texture. It is exposed in only a few places on the southeast edge of the park down by Raven Fork, Big Cove, and Maggie Valley. On top of this "basement rock" is the rock that accounts for most of the mountain mass, a collection called the Ocoee Supergroup. Tens of thousands of feet of sediments make up the Ocoee. Through its long life it's been deeply buried, folded, faulted, and baked — in the words of the geologist, metamorphosed.

The Ocoee's dominant member is the Great Smoky Group, which geologists have described as "a thick monotonous mass of clastic sedimentary rocks, pebble conglomerate, coarse to fine sandstone, and silty or argillaceous rocks." Basically muds, sands, and gravels laid down in a big ocean 600 to 900 million years ago. The Great Smoky Group is what you see all along the Newfound Gap Road, from Sugarlands in Tennessee over to Smokemont in North Carolina.

In truth, it is pretty monotonous as far as rocks go. No fossils, no nothing, mostly cleaved dark gray chunks, splattered with shocking yellow lichens and draped with emerald mosses. But a lovely section is laid bare near Newfound Gap and on the higher ridges. It's the Anakeesta Formation, tawny, rust-colored rock rich in sulfides. Sometimes fools find gold in it. Old-timers called the Anakeesta slaterock. They applied common, earthy names to others: graybacks, flintrock, and dirtrock.

Once the rock is laid down, then something must raise it up to these awesome heights. In the Smokies, the story goes that the mountains were built when two big continental plates crashed together, pretty well crumpling and pushing up the intervening land — voilà the Appalachian Mountains, of which the Smokies are the southern end. Beyond this, things get a little hypothetical. Geologists are still searching for the welt, or suture line, that would mark the tumultuous joining of the two continents. So far, they haven't found it. Throw in a fault here and a fold there, and the Smoky Mountains become hard mountains to read.

The Smokies are among the highest mountains in the East, boasting twelve peaks towering 6,000 feet or higher. They once stood much higher, and in their younger days were even more steep and rugged. Over millions of years they've been smoothed by the hands of water, wind, and ice.

The finishing touches were added during the last ice age, when the environment here was more like Canada or Alaska. Though glaciers didn't actually reach this far south, the ground

was frozen year-round and the highest peaks were more like the Rockies, with snowfields and alpine tundra.

By about 10,000 years ago the glaciers slunk off to the north, and the Smoky Mountains started to become the more temperate place we know today. That little bit of Canada — the spruce-fir forest — found refuge at the highest elevations of the Smokies, while glorious rich hardwood forests covered the coves and the valleys.

Thanks to a happy combination of the mild climate, along with plentiful rainfall and the mountains' venerable age and extreme terrain, the Great Smokies now support a diversity of plants and animals nearly unsurpassed in the temperate regions of this continent.

Gravity, water, ice, and vegetation are all forces that constantly shape and reshape the land.

Some of the park's most interesting geological features are also favorite destinations for hikers. OPPOSITE PAGE: *Alum Cave Bluff.* ABOVE AND LEFT: *Charlies Bunion.*

Black Bears

Vegetation makes up most of a black bear's diet. Favorite foods include: NEAR LEFT, *acorns,* BELOW, *black cherries and* BOTTOM, *squawroot.*

*I*t's September in the Smokies. Broad-winged hawks rocket over the ridges on their southward migrations. Sweet huckleberries hang on the bushes in the highlands. Leaves on the sumac have turned to a deep wine. Brook trout are preparing to spawn in the streams. Summer heat still simmers in the valleys.

For the black bears of the mountains, it's the time of the fall shuffle. The word "shuffle," though, fails to adequately describe their activity. The bears are frantically combing the woods around-the-clock for food. For the next couple of months every bear, old and young, male and female, will be searching out hard mast — acorns from the oaks and nuts from the hickories — along with what berries are left in the woods. This is the time when a black bear will founder on food — adding three to five pounds a day to its weight.

All of this conspicuous consumption is in preparation for winter, when the fattened, sleek bears will crawl into

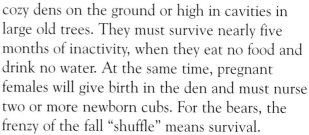

LEFT: *famed bear hunter "Black" Bill Walker and his rifle "Old Death."*

Paw print of a black bear. BELOW: *trap used for killing bears.*

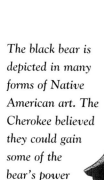

The black bear is depicted in many forms of Native American art. The Cherokee believed they could gain some of the bear's power by eating its meat.

cozy dens on the ground or high in cavities in large old trees. They must survive nearly five months of inactivity, when they eat no food and drink no water. At the same time, pregnant females will give birth in the den and must nurse two or more newborn cubs. For the bears, the frenzy of the fall "shuffle" means survival.

Native American residents of the Great Smoky Mountains, the Cherokee Indians, were keenly aware of the bears' seasonal patterns. In autumn they told stories about the bears, to them animals of immense power and sacredness. This was hunting season too, when the Cherokee would use spears, arrows, and traps to outwit these great creatures of the forest which provided them with meat, fur, and oil. In their language, the name of the bear was Yonah.

European settlers who came through the gaps to farm the fertile river valleys of the Smokies also knew the bear. Using traps, muzzle-loading rifles, and Blue Tick hounds, they tracked and hunted bears. At least two Smokies residents, "Black" Bill Walker of Tremont and "Turkey" George Palmer of Cataloochee, were legendary bear hunters — each man was said to have taken more than 100 bears.

But by 1934, when the Great Smoky Mountains became a national park, bears had become scarce. It wasn't long, though, with hunting banned and logging stopped inside the 500,000 acres of the new park, that they started to make a comeback.

The American black bear, *Ursus americanus*, ranges from Maine to Florida, to Alaska and Canada. Black bears live in the Rockies, the Sierra Nevada, and in Mexico as well. Their range is far larger and their numbers much greater than either of North America's other two species, the polar bear and the grizzly.

In the Great Smoky Mountains, black bears reach one of the highest densities anywhere on the continent.

Bears were once relatives of wild dogs, and a look at their muzzles and ears reveals that far-off evolutionary tie. But they evolved their own lineage and crossed the Bering land bridge into the New World. Black bears became strict forest dwellers, with a keen sense of smell to lead them through their treed world. Walking flat-footed along a trail on all fours, snuffing the ground, a bear can appear to be a slow, lumbering animal. But if you ever witness one running cross country or scrambling up a tree, you will come to appreciate their true agility, strength, and speed. Wildlife photographer Ken Jenkins, who has watched bears in the Smokies for many years, reports that old-timers in the mountains say "a bear can climb a tree faster than a man can fall out of one."

The black bear is the undeniable symbol of the Great Smoky Mountains, where they have found a safe sanctuary and are doing remarkably well. The park has been the site of one of the longest-running black bear research projects in the country, conducted by Dr. Michael Pelton and his graduate students from the University of Tennessee Knoxville. Every year since the early 1970s, they have been capturing, marking, and recapturing black bears. They've even tape recorded cubs in winter dens to tell how many of them there are.

The mark and recapture method is one way to count the animals. Bears are trapped, radio collars attached, and their wanderings tracked from an airplane. While not every bear is actually captured, the numbers are extrapolated to arrive at an estimate of the total population.

The other method, less expensive and labor intensive, is to set up bait, or scent, stations. For these "sardine surveys," as park biologists call them, more than 400 cans of sardines are put in trees at half-mile intervals and are then checked every five days for bear sign. The bears, attracted by the smelly fish, leave obvious traces of their presence, such as claw marks and scat. From the number of "visits" to these stations, biologists gain another measure of how many bears live in the park.

For years, the black bear population in Great Smoky Mountains National Park was said to range from 400 to 600 animals, sometimes 500 to 700. But in the 1990s, several good natural food years and other factors resulted in a significant increase in the bear population. By the late 1990s bear researchers had elevated their estimates, placing the number closer to 1,700 animals, a crowded two bears per square mile.

The Smokies offer a cornucopia of food for the omnivorous bears. When they emerge from the dens in spring, lean and hungry, they find new green grass, leaves, squawroot, and ripening serviceberries. As summer progresses, the groceries keep coming — buckets of berries and grapes, yellowjackets and other insects, and the occasional deer fawn. In past autumns American chestnut trees furnished a plentiful — and reliable — supply of nuts.

Now the picture is more complicated. With the chestnuts wiped out by blight, black bears have substituted acorns, of red and white oaks especially, for their crucial fall nutrition. Oaks, however, don't produce nuts every year as the chestnuts did. In a good mast year, everybody is fat and happy. But in the inevitable bad years, when the acorn crop fails, bears roam beyond the park boundaries in search of food, where they are not as well protected from hunting and where development is increasingly closing them out.

Always, the sight of a bear in the Smokies is a heart-stopping experience. You're driving along the loop road in Cades Cove on a tranquil morning, say, and you see two black shapes up in a tree far out in a meadow. Suddenly traffic comes to a halt and you find yourself in the middle of one of those famous Smokies "bear jams." Or, you're happily snuggled down for the night in your tent at the campground. Just as you're drifting off to sleep, you hear snuffling around the

It's easy for us to view bears as cute or clownish, but it's important to remember they are actually very powerful animals intent on the difficult job of survival.

tent. It's a skunk, you hope, but it *could* be a bear. The thought of a very thin sheet of nylon between you and a 200-pound bruin is less than comforting.

Bears and people do meet each other in the Smokies, sometimes to the detriment of both. Park rangers document hundreds of "bear incidents" each year, usually a bear rifling a picnic site, burglarizing vehicles, or marauding in a backcountry camp. In rare instances, a bear has injured a person.

In almost every case, it is human food that bears are after. They learn quickly to associate people with potato chips, hot dogs, and candy bars, a most dangerous connection for them to make. At first, a bear will be out at night looking for goodies. Then it becomes bolder and enters a picnic area in the daytime. This is the bear of greatest concern to park biologists.

Such "nuisance" bears were captured and taken many miles away to another part of the park. But bears are smart. They come back. A newer strategy is to capture "night-active" bears and perform a general biological work-up on them. The tranquilized bear is laid out on a table and weighed, measured, and marked, then returned to the same site where it was caught. The hope is that the bear will have bad memories of the place and will not be anxious to visit again. Preliminary statistics indicate this method is working.

One bear had a truly bad day when it was rifling through a dumpster in Cades Cove. The garbage truck arrived and the driver, unaware of the bear's presence, summarily emptied the dumpster's contents and proceeded to compact the trash several times during his run. Only when he disgorged the load at the landfill was his unintended passenger detected. The badly bruised bear was examined by a veterinarian and, after a week of care, was released back in the park. However, this is decidedly not an aversive technique bear managers intend to pursue.

Bear management boils down to people management. The park is making a concerted effort to keep the bears safe from us. Campers, hikers, and picnickers are implored to keep clean campsites and stow all food — every innocent scrap and morsel — and all food containers out of sight, locked in the trunk. In addition, back-country campsites — 100 of them — are equipped with a specially designed cable and pulley system by which campers suspend their food high above ground and out of a hungry bear's reach.

It's September in the Smokies. If all is well, the black bears will find plenty of acorns to eat and will enter their dens ready for a long winter's rest. With some help, they will always find in these mountains a place to roam, to raise young, to live their lives as noble wild animals.

The black bear is indeed the symbol of the Great Smoky Mountains and bear mementos abound in shops around the national park.

Creatures Great and Small

The Smokies are renowned for their amazing diversity of life. CLOCKWISE FROM ABOVE: *raccoon, land snail, northern copperhead, Argiope spider.* OPPOSITE PAGE: *white-tailed deer.*

A Ruffed Grouse explodes from the ground on the trail to Gregory Bald. A woodchuck watches from a mound beside the road around Cades Cove. A swallowtail butterfly dances in the mist of a waterfall. A white-tailed deer tiptoes down the bank of the Little River for a drink. Fireflies flash their yellow lights on a warm summer evening. A gray fox pounces on a mouse in a meadow. A red squirrel scampers down a fallen log barking furiously at an interloper. The Smoky Mountains are an ark for these and hundreds of other creatures great and small.

Then, often in the middle of the night, a Barred Owl calls out. Anyone who's camped in the Smokies has likely heard the catchy call: *who cooks for you? who cooks for you all?* This brown-eyed owl may even be heard in the daytime up in a dim cove, out looking for mice, chipmunks, foxes, flying squirrels, small birds, snails, salamanders, snakes, and insects to eat.

Many species of migratory birds from Central and South America join the Smokies' permanent residents during the summer breeding season.

CLOCKWISE FROM TOP: *Nashville Warbler, Eastern Bluebird, Northern Bobwhite, Hooded Warbler, Cedar Waxwing, Ruby-throated Hummingbird, Eastern Screech Owl.*

The Barred Owl is one of about sixty birds that reside year-round in the Smokies. Ruffed Grouse, Pileated Woodpeckers, Carolina Wrens, cardinals, crows, robins, and Blue Jays also stick around. But the rest of the park's 240 bird species come and go in a seasonal ebb and flow that crescendos in springtime, when songbirds return. Among the avian harbingers of spring, arriving from mid-March to mid-April, are the Louisiana Waterthrush and Blackburnian Warbler. They are part of a wave of "neotropical migrants," birds that winter in Mexico and Central and South America but fly north to breed and nest. They travel in flocks, airborne for hundreds of miles over the Caribbean and Gulf of Mexico, often moving at night and navigating by the stars.

On a calm April morning, the dawn chorus is almost deafening. Male Scarlet Tanagers and Indigo Buntings flash through the trees like bright ribbons, singing their hearts out to attract mates and stake out territory. To even the most casual listener, the Black-throated Green Warbler's repeated *zee zee zee zoo zay* is an unmistakable sound of the season. Joining in harmony are Ovenbirds, White-eyed and Red-eyed vireos, and a host of other warblers — black-throated blue, chestnut-sided, hooded, and parula.

Some songbirds spend the summer in the park, while others continue north. But by September, the Solitary Vireos are getting ready to leave, nipping off the succulent orange berries on the mountain ash. And by October most of the songbirds, with hawks and other raptors as well, have departed. A few, like the Carolina Junco, don't spend the energy to migrate hundreds or thousands of miles, but instead take advantage of the 5,000-foot elevation difference in the mountains and simply move down to the lowlands for the winter.

Three-fourths of all bird species in the old-growth cove hardwood forests of the Smokies are neotropical migrants. Everywhere they are being monitored because of an overall disturbing decline in their numbers. The decline may be due to disappearing rainforests in the tropics where the birds winter, or fragmentation of their forest habitat here. Preliminary research indicates that the large swath of intact deciduous forest in the Smokies may provide a crucial refuge for a number of threatened species.

While birds are vocal and visible, salamanders keep a low profile. In the Smoky Mountains, salamanders reach astounding abundance and diversity, accounting for more biomass than birds and mammals put together.

At last count, the number of salamander species in the Smokies was thirty, with new kinds still being discovered. They live in water and on land, from valleys to mountaintops. Some have lungs, some do not. They range in size from the outlandish hellbender to the inch-and-one-half pigmy salamander. The hellbender is one you wouldn't want your sister to go out on a date with. Usually about a foot and half in length, a nearly thirty-inch-long specimen was fetched from the Little Pigeon River years ago.

As amphibians, salamanders must keep their skin moist; they don't wander too far in the sunshine. Some species return each year to limestone sinkholes to lay their eggs. Marbled and spotted do so, but the marbled gets a head start by arriving in the fall instead of spring. A "breeding congress" of marbled salamanders converges at a dry pond, mates, lays eggs, then waits for the pond to fill with water.

These and other salamanders engage in creative courtship behavior, including teeth biting, chin rubbing, and tail straddling, all of which seem necessary to set the right mood and assure procreation.

Salamanders are secretive beings, spending most of their time under rocks and logs, emerging at dark. A nighttime foray along a creek or in the woods after a summer rain should yield plenty of sightings. A few are out in the daytime but they're hard to see. Hiking a trail, one gets the sense that many eyes are watching.

Special sensory organs let salamanders detect vibrations in the environment. They also have a keen sense of smell, but they cannot hear. To protect themselves, salamanders exude noxious skin secretions that taste so bad a bird will spit one out if it catches it. A snake will find its mouth glued together if it tries to eat one. Should a predator nip off a salamander's tail, it

CLOCKWISE FROM BELOW: *Red-spotted Newt, Black-chinned Red Salamander, Red-cheeked Salamander.*

can readily grow a new one.

The red-cheeked is found only in the Great Smoky Mountains. It's a lungless salamander that lives on land, probably descended from a group that started out many millions of years ago in the cold streams of the Appalachian Mountains. Lungless salamanders possess neither lungs nor gills, but instead breathe through their mouths and skin.

Salamanders, and their frog and toad kin, are critical links in the food chain — serving sometimes as predator, sometimes as prey. Because of this key ecological role, noticeable declines in

CLOCKWISE FROM ABOVE: *bobcat, radio-collared elk, red fox.*

their numbers are of concern. Over five years, scientist James Petranka documented a 50 percent drop in wood frogs in the Smokies. He is reluctant to name a cause yet, because it could be part of a natural cycle. But worldwide, biologists are sounding a real alarm about increasing deformities and decreasing populations among amphibians, salamanders included. Prime suspects are loss of habitat, acid rain, chemicals, parasites, ultraviolet radiation, or a combination of these factors. The final word is yet to come, but Smokies salamanders could prove good barometers.

A few large mammals native to the Smokies have vanished from the scene. When the first European settlers arrived, woodland bison, elk, and wolves roamed the mountains. But things changed in a hurry. All three were extirpated from the southern Appalachians, but serious steps have been taken, or are underway, to bring some of them back.

A high-profile attempt to reintroduce the red wolf ended in failure. Between 1991 and 1996, thirty-seven wolves were released into Cades Cove and the Tremont area. The hope was that Great Smoky Mountains National Park would be big enough, and the land secure and untouched enough, to harbor these endangered wolves again. Early signs were encouraging: the wolves bore young, hunted their own food, and howled to each other at night. But after eight years the project ended because too many pups and adults had died, and because the wolves failed to establish home ranges in the park.

Nearly thirty wolf pups were born during that time but few, if any, survived even a year. Biologists suspect the pups died from canine disease, parasites, predation, and malnutrition. From tracking the radio-collared adults, biologists know they died in fights with other wolves, from drinking antifreeze, and in one case, by a poacher's gun.

Early concerns that the wolves would make domestic livestock a big part of their diet did not bear out. Mostly they ate deer, raccoons, and rabbits, but the supply of natural prey in the park may have been inadequate to sustain them. Wolves that wandered onto private land had to be recaptured.

The attempt to reestablish a population of the endangered red wolf in the Smokies just didn't work. The missing link was the animals' failure, for whatever reason, to rear young successfully. Biologists were forced to recapture the handful of wolves left in the park. The U.S. Fish and Wildlife Service is evaluating other parts of the wolves' former range in the Southeast where they could be reestablished. Meanwhile, another group of red wolves is doing fine in northeast North Carolina.

In 2001 the park service initiated an experimental elk reintroduction program by importing twenty-seven elk to Cataloochee Valley. Additional animals have been trucked in and released since. As a result, visitors to Cataloochee have witnessed elk calves bounding through the fields and antlered bulls bugling into the night. During the experimental phase, the animals are radio collared so researchers can study their habits.

Local bird watchers have been elated to learn that after more than fifty years, Peregrine Falcons have once again set up housekeeping in the park. In the mid 1980s, then-endangered peregrines were released in the Smokies. By the end of the 1990s, a pair had nested and raised chicks three years in a row, the first occurrences in the Smokies since 1942. In the fall, these swift falcons may depart for Central or South America. But because peregrines mate for life and often return to the same nest year after year, the hope is that the pair will continue to show up in the Smokies each spring and bear young.

The number one wildlife pest is the wild hog, an animal not native to the Smoky Mountains. The same species as domestic pigs, wild hogs were introduced into a North Carolina game preserve in 1912. They escaped, went forth and multiplied, and migrated into the Smokies, doing lots of damage along the way.

A wild hog will eat everything from four feet high down to the ground, digging and rooting, causing erosion and silting of streams and springs, and generally creating havoc. They inhabit nearly all elevations, but their worst rooting is in the beech-birch forests in the higher terrain. In six months a 125-pound hog can consume half a ton of nuts, and in lean mast years they may compete with bears and other animals for this valuable food source. So for close to four decades rangers have trapped and shot hogs in an effort to control them. A few hundred still remain in the park, and may always be here.

'Possums, moles, voles, mice, squirrels, bats, beetles, spiders, snakes, ants, and yes even fleas — the Smokies ark protects all that belong, no matter how great or small.

Discovering Life

Here's what we know lives in the Smoky Mountains: nearly 450 species of vertebrates, 4,280 species of invertebrates, 2,800 species of plants, and 2,000 species of fungi. As astounding as those figures are, scientists estimate that is only about ten percent of what's actually here.

To try to discover the full range of life in the park, Great Smoky Mountains has become the site of the All Taxa Biodiversity Inventory, ATBI for short. The project, the nation's first, hopes to accomplish nothing short of identifying every higher life form in the park — every millipede, spider, fungus, fish, butterfly, salamander — possibly more than 100,000 species in all.

ATBI is not just another government program. Over the next ten to fifteen years specialists, teachers, students, retirees, anyone who wants to volunteer in this effort is invited. Comprehensive checklists, range maps, and basic natural history information are the specific inventory goals. To distribute the findings as widely as possible, various media, including a World Wide Web site, will be updated frequently.

As exciting as the task will be, it holds some urgency because of threats to the park's ecosystems, mostly from outside influences — air pollution, exotic plants and animals, and development around the park.

For information on ATBI, contact the park or check the website at www.discoverlife.org.

Wildwood

Naturalist John Muir (below) walked the length of the Appalachian Range and raised awareness of the human need

for wild places and virgin forests. ABOVE RIGHT: *flowering dogwood in April woods.* RIGHT: *Pileated Woodpecker.* OPPOSITE PAGE: *a circle of American basswood trees.*

Entering the Albright Grove is like going into a cathedral. Here in the presence of ancient, majestic trees we may worship and learn patience and humility.

The grove is reached by walking a few miles up the Maddron Bald Trail. First it's an old road, lined with creamy white flowering dogwoods on a spring day. Cross a footbridge over a small creek and keep walking. The road narrows to a trail, and the forest begins to feel different. The straight, even stands of tulip-trees give way to immense hardwoods: oak, cherry, maple, buckeye, and basswood. Beams of sunlight filter through the lacy branches of the eastern hemlocks in the cool ravine. Beneath the trees grow Fraser's sedge, trout lily, and partridgeberry. A woodpecker hammers away without cease in an old standing snag. In a sun-drenched patch opened by a wind-toppled giant, seedlings have taken root.

There are few places like this left in the world. This is the kind of forest naturalist John Muir marveled at throughout the Appalachian Mountains only a century ago, forest spared the logger's saw and

Champion Trees

Mature forests filled with old trees are now precious. In the East, the Great Smoky Mountains claim a large portion of the old-growth that once clothed the region. As much as a fourth of the park's acreage contains virgin trees hundreds of years old (the oldest tree known in the park is a 564-year-old black-gum). This is a forest of champions, trees so tall you can't see the tops and so great in girth it takes a group of six people joining hands to encircle them. A northern red oak 257 inches in circumference, a Carolina silverbell 155 inches, a yellow buckeye 229 inches, and a red maple 276 inches!

Besides trees of great size and age, an old-growth forest, like a healthy human community, holds young and middle-aged members too. A scattering of smaller shrubs forms an understory beneath the "ceiling" or canopy. A pandemonium of wildflowers, ferns, mosses, mushrooms, lichens, and liverworts covers the ground. Hidden from view underground is another teeming collection of life — bacteria, fungi, and tiny soil animals — helping decompose plant material and recycle nutrients, vital services for this complex ecosystem we call a forest.

farmer's plow. Muir wrote in 1898 that he wished for one more chance before he died to salute these "grand, godly" trees.

Sometimes forests can be taken for granted, like air and water. We see them all the time and so sometimes fail to notice them. But consider that trees consist chemically of much the same things we do. Like us they are born, grow, reproduce, and die. And like us, no two are alike.

A forest and its trees feed and shelter birds, insects, and mammals. Trees provide shade, hold soil on hillsides, deliver water, and prevent floods. They make their own food by combining sunlight with green chlorophyll, sugar, and carbon. In this process of photosynthesis, they give off oxygen, without which we would not be here. As one biologist astutely observed, trees are the "lung tissue" of the earth.

Most of the nearly 100 species of native trees of the Smokies forests belong to the broad-leaved, deciduous category. After a summer of prodigious growth, deciduous trees enter a time of quiet. The habit of dropping their leaves lets the trees conserve water during the cold, dry winter. The deciduous forest passes through a distinct annual cycle — in spring the trees flower and buds unfurl, painting the forest in soft hues of chartreuse, lime, and gray-green. The leafing out leaps up the mountainsides like wildfire. Through the summer, the Smokies forest is a tunnel of solid, dark green, the canopy and understory so thick the sky is closed off. In autumn, the forest transforms into a riotous palette of orange, yellow, red, scarlet, purple, and gold. In winter, when the leaves have fallen to the ground, the mountains are cloaked in a furwrap of brown and gray and the elegant geometry of individual trees is exposed.

How did this forest come to be so rich? First, the climate is temperate and moisture is abundant

— precipitation averages sixty inches a year but approaches ninety inches at the highest places. Plants love this moisture and humidity. They soak it up and give it back with profligacy. Competition here is not for water, but for space and light.

The mountainous terrain provides an almost infinite number of nooks and crannies for plants to occupy. Varied temperatures, well-developed soil, and microhabitats support the vast variety of vegetation. Also, these mountains have been here a long, long time, free of oceans or ice sheets for millions of years. During the period when cool glacial air breathed down the neck of the southern Appalachians, northern-style spruce and fir moved southward, replacing hardwoods on lower slopes, while alpine tundra held the summits. The hardwood trees and other plant species took refuge in the warmer valleys. Once conditions warmed again, those remnants were waiting in the wings to reoccupy habitat once again hospitable to them.

The cove hardwood forests of the southern Appalachians are the richest of the rich. These are sheltered stands that grow on moist, deep-soiled hillsides below elevations of 4,500 feet, the places that harbored deciduous hardwoods during glacial times. Within a quarter acre of cove hardwood forest grow sixty or seventy species of vascular plants, compared to only about thirty species in an "average" eastern deciduous forest of equal size.

The trees you will find here are white basswood, yellow birch, beech, yellow buckeye, silverbell, tuliptree, sugar maple, black locust, and hickory, among others. They're tall and stately, their uppermost branches towering 150 feet overhead. In springtime, fringed phacelia whitens the ground, in summer black snakeroot is common, and in the fall yellow jewelweed dazzles the slopes. Giant boulders, festooned with flourescent green moss, clog the ravines, the rocks old-timers called graybacks. These magnificent cove hardwood forests are nearly unequaled in diversity

Many components make up the rich diversity of forest life.
CLOCKWISE FROM TOP: *redbud tree, fly agaric mushrooms, beech forest, sugar maple trees, deer mouse.*

and productivity on this continent.

But that's not all the Smokies' forest types. Between 3,000 to 5,000 feet elevation grows the northern hardwood forest. Though not as

diverse as the cove hardwood type, it is unique as the highest-elevation, broad-leaved forest in the East. The dominant species are yellow birch and American beech, distinguished in a couple of ways. Yellow birch is wrapped in shimmery, paper-thin bark,

and individual trees are often propped on exposed roots as if standing on stilts. American beech can be told by the crinkled brown leaves that hang from the branches all winter; this is the tree that produces brown beech-nuts savored by all kinds of wildlife.

The northern

hardwoods butt up against the culminating forest type — the spruce and fir trees at the highest elevations of the park. Here it's almost always cool and often windy, the evergreens growing on the mist-shrouded crest of the mountains, the trees skimmed with hoarfrost in winter, the trails deep in snow. Where birds like Red Crossbills and saw-whet owls, and mammals like the northern flying squirrel, can be found. Where tufts of glistening club moss,

TOP: *a Red-tailed Hawk watches an opening in the forest canopy for prey.* ABOVE: *the park's evergreen spruce-fir forests occur at the highest elevations.*

lovely northern lady ferns, and pink-flowered Catawba rhododendrons add beauty and variety. Where spring's tardy arrival is marked by the appearance of patches of dainty little spring-beauties. It's all a touch of Labrador here in the Smokies.

The spruce-fir forest, an ice-age relict, has survived in the southern Appalachians as a handful of "islands" separated from one another and from the true boreal forest much farther north. This forest accounts for only about two percent of the park acreage, but contributes great interest and diversity. These isolated "islands" support botanical rarities, including endemics found only in this forest. Rugel's rag-wort is one, along with Cain's reedgrass and Appalachian avens growing on Mount Le Conte.

The two main trees are Fraser fir and red spruce. Like all the clan, the fir bears upright cones on the branches, while spruce cones hang down like pendants. Fir needles are blunt and flat, and the milky white resinous blisters on the bark inspired the appellation "she-balsam" among the mountaineers.

The mood of the spruce-fir forest today is sad and eerie. A non-native insect, the balsam wool-ly adelgid, has sucked the life from the Fraser fir, leaving only denuded trunks, stripped of all foliage, standing like phantoms among the black-green spruce. The adelgid, introduced in the early part of the twentieth century from Europe, was carried south by the wind along the Appalachians. It arrived in the Smokies in 1963, and has since killed nearly all the mature Fraser fir. There is little hope that the insect can be controlled or that the fir will come back. With one of the two dominant species gone, the ecolo-gy of the spruce-fir forest is likely undergoing significant alterations, many of which won't be apparent for years.

Existing in stark contrast to the tangle of green forests are the mysterious openings called balds. An easy one to get to is Andrews Bald, a two-mile hike from Clingmans Dome. From the rocky, root-buckled trail through the dark woods you emerge suddenly into a world of light. The bald is a meadow of mountain oat grass, golden in the fall, surrounded by hawthorns and huckleberry bushes bearing a few last fruits. On the edges are fading purple gentians and the dry seedheads of wild carrot. Clouds waft in and out, leaving you in a small private world.

No one can say for certain why Andrews Bald and several others in the Smokies exist. They are treeless areas, occurring mostly on ridge tops between 5,000 and 6,000 feet. Cold and exposure, herds of elk and bison, and grazing livestock have all been invoked to explain them. The Cherokee say the Great Spirit sent down a bolt of lightning to kill an enemy, and henceforth the high mountains would remain treeless.

Heath balds are another type, different from grassy balds in their plant life and probably their origin. These "hells" or "slicks," as mountain people call them, consist of low-growing, shiny-leaved shrubs that are impenetrable to anyone on foot. Among them are the beautiful flowering rhododendron, azalea, sand myrtle, mountain laurel, and berry bushes. Heath balds occur most often on steep west-facing slopes, and botanists speculate that fire may maintain them.

From the curious balds to the rich old-growth forests, the Smoky Mountains exhibit nearly infinite botanical wealth. We have only to go and see it, and count ourselves blessed.

Treeless areas called heath balds are common in the Smokies. From a distance they appear smooth and shiny and are sometimes called "slicks."

Great pleasure can be derived from driving one of the park's backroads like Balsam Mountain. The leisurely pace on these unpaved routes allows time to revel in the Smokies' smaller wonders, such as: mushrooms, partridge berry, lichens, and ground-nesting birds.

Every April people flock to the Great Smoky Mountains to enjoy one of the most varied and beautiful wildflower displays on our planet.
CLOCKWISE FROM LEFT: *white trillium, Jack-in-the-pulpit, Goldfinch, fringed phacelia, small purple-fringed orchid.*

On a warm, rainy spring morning, a mother and daughter stroll down the Ramsey Cascades Trail, walking sticks in hand, stopping to tell complete strangers about an exciting wildflower they've just seen. Cleverly camouflaged beneath the leaves of another plant, it's a Jack-in-the-pulpit — "Jack" hidden under a striped hood. They were especially delighted with their find, for Mom recalled hiking to the falls many years ago, and this was the first time she'd been back.

The Smoky Mountains are like that. Even after a long absence, they tug at the heart strings, especially in springtime when the great flowering occurs. Along with Jack-in-the-pulpit are hundreds of other wildflowers blooming in a floral extravaganza.

For some, fond memories of trilliums dancing on the hillsides bring them back year after year. Ten species of these lovely lilies are known in the park, including the big-blossomed white trillium, the lemon-scented yellow trillium, the deep maroon wake robin, and the painted

Learning to name some of the park's common wildflowers is one of the joys of a trip to the Smokies. A wide range of learning opportunities are available, including the Wildflower Pilgrimage held each April.

LEFT SIDE OF PAGE, FROM TOP: *false Solomon's seal, fall asters, bloodroot, budding botanists, purple phacelia.*

RIGHT SIDE OF PAGE, FROM TOP: *showy orchis, columbine, foamflower, fire pink, squirrel corn, and mountain spiderwort.*

30

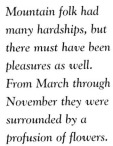

Mountain folk had
many hardships, but
there must have been
pleasures as well.
From March through
November they were
surrounded by a
profusion of flowers.

Mountain folk often planted domestic plants around their homes, like this day lily at the Noah "Bud" Ogle farmstead on Cherokee Orchard Road.

trillium's filmy white flower scrimshawed with pink.

Earning the award of "earliest flowering wildflower in the Smokies" is trailing arbutus. The tubular white blossoms of this heath can appear in late February, usually in the drier oak-pine woods. Close behind it come other harbingers of

sunlight can still reach the forest floor.

Through March and early April, the mountains can retain a wintry visage. But by mid-April, the swiftness of the flowering is mind boggling. Each day brings something new. By word-of-mouth, through an amazingly efficient informal grapevine, people share news of another floral find. Dutchman's breeches on the parkway,

spring: bloodroot, hepatica, and phacelia. Before the trees have leafed out, these beauties broadcast the glad tidings that winter is over. A short walk up the Bradley Fork, Porters Creek, or Chestnut Top trails will reward wildflower seekers with the sight of cheery "prevernal" flowers, poking up through the layers of dry leaves while

delicate bleeding heart along the Little River Road, a pink lady's slipper on the Cosby Nature Trail, dwarf crested iris down at Metcalf Bottoms. Mayapples, violets, Solomon's seal, bishop's cap, bluets. Keep looking, and there's a cut-leaved toothwort, a rue anemone, a trout-lily, and lo and behold, a whorled pogonia!

But look up too. During springtime, the other flowering plants — trees and shrubs — are also blooming. Everybody knows and loves the dogwood and the redbud when they bloom. With them are the starry white flowers of serviceberry, or "sarvice" as it's called, because it bloomed about the time the circuit riding preacher came around in spring to perform baptisms and marriages. One April day a Carolina silverbell along the Little River Road suddenly explodes with exquisite, white, bell-shaped flowers. And the common tuliptree becomes a little less common when it produces generous, tulip-shaped, yellow and orange flowers.

This is the time of an annual Smokies ritual — the Spring Wildflower Pilgrimage. For several days in late April, people caravan through the park to see the amazing display, while photographers buzz around the flowers like bees.

Arthur Stupka, park naturalist for nearly twenty-five years, faithfully recorded the seasonal happenings in his journal. In some years, it was tough to keep up with the pace of nature. Mr. Stupka pioneered the "Bloomin' Report" which chronicled weekly wildflower sightings.

The wonderful thing about the mountains is you can follow spring upward, finding things in bloom around the heights of Balsam Mountain and Newfound Gap that have already had their day down in the valleys.

By May and June, the woods are a wall of green. The trees are fully leafed out, and so the sun-loving wildflowers taper off. But don't despair. It's time to head to the heath balds and ogle the delectable mountain laurel blossoms. The rhododendrons are also coming on — the abundant rosebay with waxy white flowers, and the Catawba's profuse, breathtaking purple-pink blossoms. From early to mid June, the Alum Cave Bluffs Trail is a favorite place to see Catawba rhododendron in full glory. Toward the middle and end of June, the hike to view the flame azaleas on Gregory Bald is another celebrated summer ritual. The great plant man William Bartram described the azalea colors as the "finest red lead, orange and bright gold, as

well as yellow and cream," sometimes all these shades appearing on the same plant.

As summer slips away, the flowers that remain are those that can grow tall toward the sun — goldenrod, ironweed, Joe-pye-weed, lobelia, and asters. But as surely as the seasons tick by, we have only to wait for flowerland's arrival next spring.

The Smokies are cloaked with a spectacular array of flowering shrubs. ABOVE AND INSET: *Catawba rhododendron.* LEFT: *flame azalea.*

Branches, Prongs, and Forks

The water in park streams is some of the purest in America. It is also teeming with life, some of which provides food for both human and beast. OPPOSITE PAGE: *Little Pigeon River.*

On a sultry Sunday afternoon in the Smokies, the best place to be is by a cool, flowing stream. Lower Abrams Creek, at the far western edge of the park, fits the bill. A fisherman whiles away the afternoon in the quiet campground, nobody else much around. Suddenly, something catches his eye, and he's up and running excitedly alongside the creek. He motions a hiker over to take a look too.

It's four sleek river otters, diving and swimming in the chocolate-gray water. As soon as the quartet sees the people, they're gone, slipping out of sight underwater, declining to surface again. A daytime appearance of these graceful, aquatic mammals is indeed a breathtaking sight.

It is heartwarming to see these beautiful animals once again swimming and cavorting in the creeks of the Smokies. Gone when the park was established in the 1930s, victims of trapping and logging, river otters have made a comeback. In 1986, eleven of them were

A hike in the Great Smoky Mountains will usually take you along, over, and through some of the park's glittering streams. You'll be tempted to dabble your toes in the chilly waters and press your fingertips into the spongy mats of moss.
OPPOSITE PAGE: *Tom Branch Falls.*

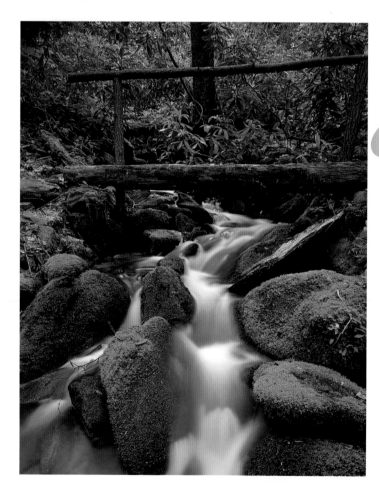

reintroduced into lower Abrams Creek, where deep pools and limpid water proved good habitat. When otters find what they need — shelter, plenty of fish to eat, and other otters to socialize with — they form what biologists call strong "site attachments." That's just what happened in Abrams Creek.

Since that initial release, over another ten years nearly 140 otters have been introduced into drainages throughout park, and they have settled in. Otters appear to have become permanently reestablished in their native waters.

To the good fortune of river otters and all kinds of aquatic creatures, Great Smoky Mountains National Park boasts more than 2,000 miles of flowing streams. Here they are better known as branches, prongs, and forks: Parson Branch, Kephart Prong, Roaring Fork, to name a few.

The soothing sound of a laughing stream drowns out other cares. Sit and listen and you'll hear the rocks rolling along, having a conversation among themselves. A kingfisher dives into the foam, nabs a fish, and takes it back to the tree branch to consume it. A water strider sculls furiously across the surface of a calm pool. A sycamore leaf spirals down and lazes away on the current. Hours slip by as you watch, mesmerized by the energy of flowing water and its determined, unstoppable movement.

From their headwaters in the highest elevations, streams tumble down steep hillsides, rush over boulders, thread through fallen trees. Swollen with rainfall, especially during the wettest months of March and July, creeks roar downslope, scouring channels and slowing only when they get to the flatter, lower reaches. All are headed inexorably for the Tennessee River and finally the Gulf of Mexico.

Streams are tied intimately to the land through which they pass. Rock and soil profoundly influence water chemistry and sediment loads. Waters nourish the roots of the elegant, alabaster-barked sycamore trees. In turn, the forest feeds streams with leaves drifting down from overhanging trees. In autumn, especially, a big pulse of leaf fall enters the creeks and rivers. This is a major source of nutrition for stream-dwelling creatures that proceed to pierce, scrape, and shred the leaves into smaller pieces.

Everything about a stream ecosystem is adapted to moving water. Strands of green mosses — fountain moss, beard moss, cedar moss, and plume moss — cling to boulders in the cool running water. Aquatic insects find shelter within the tangled mass of the moss, in the leaf pack, and under rocks. Separate the filaments of moss and you'll likely find mayfly larvae. Mayflies are ephemeral creatures. They live as aquatic nymphs, and when they hatch into adults they take to the air to perform nuptial flights that last only a day or two. Then they die. When swarms of mayflies cloud the air in April and May, anglers grab their fly rods and hurry to the streams intent on hooking trout.

Turn over a rock in a stream and you may see a stonefly nymph. Or curious little cases of woven sticks, pebbles, and grains of sand attached to the rock. These are the architectural creations of caddisfly larvae. The cases, in the forms of funnel-shaped nets, snails, or shells, are ingeniously designed to capture edible morsels floating downstream.

The crayfish or "river lobster," serves as the backbone of the stream food chain — savored by frogs, fish, raccoons, and otters. A notable streamside bird is the nattily dressed Belted Kingfisher. As the bird's name implies, fish are its favored food, especially big minnows called stonerollers. Smokies streams exhibit an amazingly diverse fish collection — along with stonerollers are sculpins, shiners, suckers, chubs, daces, darters, and madtoms.

And there are trout. Herein lies a story of

Falling Waters

The spell of moving water is irresistible. And nowhere is that spell so strong as by a waterfall. These jewels, set deep in the Smokies woods, are veils of foam cascading down stairstep boulders, threads of silver in heavenly glens adorned with emerald moss, fountains of cool spray.

Waterfalls are as close as the nearest roadway, or as far as an all-day hike. Laurel Falls is one of the easiest to reach. The trailhead is about four miles from the Sugarlands Visitor Center. It is a mile-and-a-third walk on a paved trail beside Laurel Branch, clothed with namesake mountain laurel bushes in pink-blush bloom in May. A narrow rock ledge through a tunnel of trees leads to the breathtaking view of the eighty-foot falls.

Roaring Fork Motor Nature Trail on the edge of Gatlinburg leads to several waterfalls. Grotto Falls is only about a mile and a half up

the Trillium Gap Trail, past massive virgin hemlocks along the way. You can hear the falls before you see them. Rainbow Falls is a longer hike, two and a half miles with a 1,500-foot rise in elevation. Farther along the motor nature trail, right beside the road, is the impressive Place of a Thousand Drips.

From Cosby Campground, the Gabes Mountain Trail follows Crying Creek for a couple of miles, with a detour down to Hen Wallow Falls, ninety feet high.

Over on the North Carolina side of the park, a walk of less than a mile up Deep Creek takes you to Indian Creek and Tom Branch falls, delightful places to cool off on a hot summer day.

One of the longest, and most beautiful, hikes is to Ramsey Cascades. From the trailhead in the Greenbrier area, it's a solid four-mile uphill walk through an inspiring old-growth forest. The awesome 100-foot-high cascade at trail's end rewards your efforts and renews your soul.

And remember, besides renewing your soul you'll want to watch out for your body. The moss- and algae-covered rocks around waterfalls are slick as ice, and can cause a person to lose footing and take a bad tumble. Use extra caution around the falls.

ABOVE: *The popular, one-and-one-third-mile hike to Laurel Falls starts from Little River Road.*
FAR RIGHT: *This view of Ramsey Cascades can be found by hiking four miles from the Ramsey Cascades trailhead at Greenbrier Cove.*

TOP LEFT: Mouse Creek Falls can be viewed from Big Creek Trail. It's two miles to the falls from Big Creek Campground.

ABOVE RIGHT: Rainbow Falls is one of the most elegant waterfalls in the Smokies. Viewing it is best after a good rain. The trail to the falls that starts from Cherokee Orchard Road near Gatlinburg is about two-and-a-half miles.

LEFT: Grotto Falls is a popular destination for hikers. The well-worn, one-and-a-half mile trail to the waterfall departs from Roaring Fork Motor Nature Trail.

BELOW: *the Little River, one of the largest and richest streams in the Great Smokies.*
OPPOSITE PAGE: *winter on the Little River.*

lost habitat and the interactions between a non-native fish and a native fish the park wants to save. Once upon a time, brook trout inhabited hundreds of miles of streams in the Smokies. Old-timers called the brook trout "spec," for lovely splotches of red and green on its body. When logging removed overhanging trees, water temperatures rose. Sediment washed off the denuded mountainsides and clogged the stream gravels where the trout spawned. And with no bag limits in the old days, too many "specs" were probably taken by people for food.

In response, brook trout retreated to the higher reaches of streams. Meanwhile, non-native rainbow trout were stocked to replace them. The rainbows spread upstream, seeming to possess a competitive edge over the smaller, more delicate brookies with their specific habitat needs. By the 1970s, the future for brook trout was dim. They were found in only about 120 miles of streams in the park, and to worsen matters, brown trout had also come in.

So, park biologists are working to restore brook trout. They electrofish stretches of stream, removing the rainbows and placing them downstream below natural barriers such as small waterfalls, which they hope the fish cannot negotiate. The job requires years of persistent and repeated effort, but results are encouraging. Brook trout have been brought back to four streams, and will be reintroduced into several more.

Three kinds of trout call the Little River home: rainbow, brown, and brook. However, only the brookie is native to the southern Appalachian Mountains. A Little River brown or rainbow trout will occasionally grow to over 20 inches long.

The fishing spider, Belted Kingfisher, and licensed flyfishermen can fish in the park all year round. During winter, however, fish and most aquatic insects reduce their levels of activity.

Down Home

Much mountain music included ballads and jigs from the British Isles.

*O*On a lazy Saturday morning in Cades Cove, the air is filled with the sweet strains of banjos, mandolins, and dulcimers. Loose-knit groups of musicians gather by a big old oak tree, under the eaves of the barn, and over yonder by the corncrib. One man saws away on a 100-year-old fiddle made by his grandfather. The toe-tapping tunes inspire one woman to get up, and with a twinkle in her eye, move to the center of the circle and take to clogging. Meanwhile, out on the porch of the Becky Cable house, a chorus sings gospel hymns in exquisite harmony. Nobody needs a song book, for everyone knows the words by heart.

Mountain music is a joyous thing. From a church pew to a front porch, music was, and is, a common denominator among Smoky Mountain folks, furnishing relief from the day-in-and-day-out hard work. Often set in a mournful minor key, music was part of the warp and weft of mountain life.

Settlers brought the songs from England, Ireland, and Scotland. But others of different heritage were here before them. By about 1000 A.D., the Cherokee Indians

Churches in the Smokies resounded with song. Mountain folk were carried on waves of music through weddings, baptisms, and funerals.

LEFT: *Cherokee leader Sequoya invented the Cherokee alphabet in 1821.*

BELOW: *a Cherokee woman pounds corn into flour using the traditional mortar and pestle.*

another, with the new United States government, ceding their lands and finally giving up the heart of the Great Smoky Mountains.

Hearing the news of newly gained territory, people in Kentucky, Virginia, and North Carolina flowed through the low gaps in the mountains, claiming the best bottomlands where they could build a log cabin and start a small farm.

The Cherokee remained on what land they had left and tried to assimilate into the conquering culture. They set up a government modeled after the federal one, and used a written language invented by the famous Sequoyah. They even served the U.S. government in the War of 1812, under then-general Andrew Jackson. Despite such loyalty and progressiveness, the Cherokee were occupying land coveted by the new settlers.

To solve the "problem," in 1838 then-president Jackson ordered their removal. In hundreds of wagons and with whatever household goods they could take, the Cherokee crossed the Mississippi River and went on to Oklahoma along what became known as the Trail of Tears. It was one of the darkest times in their history, a time still not forgotten. Traditional leaders such as Yonaguska, and others, hid in the inaccessible headwaters of their beloved Smoky Mountains. Many of their descendants now live on the Qualla Reservation bordering the southern edge of the national park.

Meanwhile, the settlers kept coming, selecting first the fertile banks of the Oconaluftee River and, by the early to mid 1800s, land in Cataloochee, Cades Cove, White Oak Flats (later called Gatlinburg), Roaring Fork valley, and Greenbrier.

The first task facing any pioneer family was to clear land and plant a corn crop. The huge trees were girdled and left to die and fall. As soon as field space was available, corn was planted and a garden was put in. By the mid-nineteenth century, nearly everybody took to growing a white field corn called Hickory King. Beyond the fields was a forest full of deer, bear, and squirrels to be hunted, and streams flush with fish.

Whatever people needed, they built or made

had established villages throughout their nation, which included the Smoky Mountains. Each village had a large meeting place, called a council house, whose layout reflected the seven clans of the Cherokee. For centuries, the Cherokee followed bison trails through the mountains, trading with other tribes. They possessed intimate knowledge of the animals and plants — stories of the origin of the bear and the healing power of snakeroot.

But by the late 1700s, the lives of the Cherokee were poised on the brink of drastic change. An onslaught of Euro-Americans was pushing westward from the seaboard colonies. New diseases and battles claimed Cherokee lives. Attempting to compromise and adapt to the newcomers, the chiefs signed treaties, one after

themselves. A few good straight tuliptrees were hewn into logs laid up in a one-room cabin — maybe 720 square feet — for mom, dad, and five or six kids. The corners were carefully notched with half-dovetails or other secure joinery that would shed water down and away from the logs. The spaces between the logs were chinked with mud, and oak was split for shingles for the roof. A small glass window was a luxurious addition.

Mountain folk maintained that a person had to build "by the signs." For example, the boards

had to be put on the house during the dark of the moon so they wouldn't curl. (Likewise, crops had to planted with the signs, to assure a good harvest.)

To meet community needs, mountaineers banded together to build turnpikes, schools, and churches. To grind corn into meal, nearly every community had a small tub mill on a creek. There were bigger mills too, like Mingus Mill near Oconaluftee and Cable Mill at Cades Cove, driven by a handmade water wheel. The miller extracted a "toll" of corn for his work, and each family went home with fresh, stone-ground cornmeal for their daily bread.

Food was plain and simple, and usually plentiful. Again, with the exceptions of a few luxuries like sugar, coffee, and salt, what mountain

During the 19th century, mountain folk produced more of life's necessities and depended less on store-bought goods. Whatever people needed, they grew, built, or made themselves.

Many rural residents had a strong sense of community. Public buildings often did double duty as schools during the week and churches on Sunday.

Families and neighbors often came together to help each other with farm work or simply to be social.
ABOVE: *folks gather to boil sorghum.*
BELOW: *the park is still the site of many family reunions.*

people ate they raised themselves. Gathering, preparing, and preserving food was almost exclusively women's work. A woman felt fortunate to graduate from hearth cooking to a Home Comfort woodstove, whose successful operation required practiced skill. Beside the stove was the meal gum, a bin that held flour or cornmeal ready to be stirred up into a mess of biscuits or cornbread on a moment's notice. A crock of pickled beans, a full "tater hole," and a good supply of sulphured apples meant a family would eat well through the winter. Out in the smokehouse hung savory country hams and slabs of bacon. For a sweet treat, a hive full of bees might furnish honey, preferably from the flowers of the sourwood tree. Honey, and apples, were important cash crops to the mountaineers. In the fall people got together for the all-day task of cooking down the juice of green sorghum cane into dark molasses.

Drink was as important as food, and to most mountain folks that meant pure spring water, essential to good health and a long life. Buttermilk and cider were often on hand too. Coffee had to be bought, but teas could be brewed from mint or sassafras root. Moonshine, a well-known but largely illicit product, was brewed from corn mash in a still tucked in a rhododendron thicket. Families often kept a jug on hand for medicinal purposes, or sold it for a little money during the Depression. So plentiful was "white lightnin" in Cosby, Tennessee, that it was known at one time as the Moonshine Capital of the World.

The utilitarian items produced by mountain folk were beautiful crafts in their own rite. A patchwork quilt let a woman express her sense of design and creativity. Handspun thread woven into an intricate coverlet became a family heirloom. Split oak baskets were exceptionally well made. Dolls of corn husks with dried apple faces, and the iron work of a talented blacksmith became trademark mountain crafts.

This self-sufficient farming life lasted through

most of the nineteenth century. But by the late 1800s, the arrival of another industry brought big changes to the mountains. The magnificent Appalachian hardwoods caught the logger's eye. For a couple of decades logging was a small-scale undertaking, the cutting done by hand with crosscut saws and the timber hauled out by mules or oxen. All that changed again in the early 1900s. Railroads were driven deep into the woods, and steam-powered skidders shuttled the logs down the slopes to booming sawmill towns like Elkmont, Townsend, and Smokemont. In another couple of decades, this industrial-scale logging left two-thirds of the land that would become the national park cut over and burned by forest fires.

Alarmed by the devastation, voices were raised in support of setting aside land as a preserve or park. One man who led the chorus was Horace Kephart, a middle-aged librarian who came to live in the isolated confines of Deep Creek. "Why," Kephart implored, "should future generations be robbed of all chance to see with their own eyes what a real forest, a real wildwood, a real unimproved work of God, is like?"

And so, in 1926 the federal government established Great Smoky Mountains National Park. The process of buying up thousands of individual, private parcels took another eight years to accomplish. Tennessee and North Carolina committed funds, as did the Rockefeller family, to finally make the purchases by 1934. The Transmountain Road was built across the park, and on Labor Day 1940, President Franklin Delano Roosevelt stood at Newfound Gap and dedicated the park.

Many people left their Smoky Mountain homes with sadness and regret. For some, it was exile from the Garden of Eden. But most of them didn't go far, and they and their descendants still come back — to get a jug of pure water from a bold spring, to catch up with friends and relatives at annual homecomings, to lay flowers on the grave of a loved one, and to sing those old mountain songs.

Apple Stack Cake

Cake making was a fine art among Smoky Mountain cooks. They had a wide repertoire of recipes, but a regional specialty was apple stack cake. This was a multilayered affair of white cake interspersed with a spiced apple spread, much like a torte.

Different people had different preferences on the apple filling. Some insisted that a proper stack cake used only dried apples, reconstituted and sweetened with molasses. Others would go with applesauce sweetened to taste and spiced with cinnamon and nutmeg.

The cake was much like a cookie dough, preferably patted into thin, perfect circles by hand. The more layers a stack cake had, the better — eight or twelve layers wouldn't be unusual. The height of the cake held social significance. Florence Cope Bush wrote that an apple stack cake was the centerpiece at her grandparents' wedding reception in 1898. Each woman contributed a layer; the higher the cake, the more prominent and popular the bride and her family.

Lois Caughron of Cades Cove gave the following recipe, from her mother Laura Anthony Shuler.

1 3/4 c. white sugar	2 eggs
1 tsp soda	1/2 tsp cinnamon
1 c. butter or	1 tsp vanilla
shortening	6 c. all-purpose
3 tsp baking powder	flour
1 1/4 c. molasses or	1/2 c. buttermilk
brown sugar	Pinch salt
1/2 tsp nutmeg	

Preheat oven to 375 degrees. Cream sugar and shortening. Add molasses, vanilla, and eggs, beat thoroughly. Sift together dry ingredients. Add alternately with milk. Divide batter into 6 equal parts and shape into 6 balls. Place into 8- or 9-inch greased, floured cake pans. Pat dough to edge or roll and cut to size. Bake 10 minutes. Cool and stack with cooked, dried apples sweetened to taste. Better after it sits a day or two.

Suggested Reading

Alsop, Fred J. III. *Birds of the Smokies*. Great
    Smoky Mountains Association,
    Gatlinburg, TN, 1991.

Frome, Michael. *Strangers in High Places*.
    University of Tennessee Press,
    Knoxville, 1966.

Heinrich, Bernd. *The Trees in My Forest*.
    Cliff Street Books, New York, 1997.

Houk, Rose. *Great Smoky Mountains
    National Park: A Natural History Guide*.
    Houghton Mifflin, Boston, 1993.

Kemp, Steve. *Trees & Familiar Shrubs of the
    Smokies*. Great Smoky Mountains
    Association, Gatlinburg, TN, 1993.

Moore, Harry L. *A Roadside Guide to the
    Geology of the Great Smoky Mountains
    National Park*. University of Tennessee
    Press, Knoxville, 1988.

Rennicke, Jeff. *The Smoky Mountain Black
    Bear: Spirit of the Hills*. Great Smoky
    Mountains Association, Gatlinburg, TN,
    1991.

Trout, Ed. *Historic Buildings of the Smokies*.
    Great Smoky Mountains Association,
    Gatlinburg, TN, 1995.

White, Peter et al. *Wildflowers of the
    Smokies*. Great Smoky Mountains
    Association, Gatlinburg, TN, 1996.